AF207646

"One of the biggest gifts we can give our adopted children is a safe place to explore difficult feelings, but it's often intimidating to start these important conversations. That's why we're thankful for *Together Forever No Matter What!* It tenderly explores these scary emotions while providing parents with the language they need to be a source of stability and safety. Every adoptive parent should own this book!"

Jimmy and Kelly Needham
Hosts of the Clearly Podcast, authors, speakers, adoptive parents

"As both an adoptee myself and the mother of adopted kids, I can highly recommend *Together Forever No Matter What* as an engaging and gentle means to open the door to tough but necessary conversations, with sweet sensitivity for the tender heart of an adopted child."

Connilyn Cossette
Christy Award Winning and ECPA best-selling author, adoptive parent

"This book not only addresses the fear children have of abandonment, but also models gracious parenting. It truly mirrors the love that God our Father has for each one of us and the fact that we all need to be reminded daily that we're loved, valued, and wanted. I believe many adoptive families will find great comfort and healing in reading this book with their children. It also has great potential to open up discussions with children who may have been afraid to say anything. I highly recommend this book for any adoptive family, no matter the age of the child!"

Trisha Porter
Chief Engagement Officer at Backyard Orphans, adoptive mom

"Charity Clayton's book *Together Forever No Matter What* has the answer to an adopted child's deepest question: 'Will you always love me?' A parent taking time to read this book out loud to their child gives them words of promise, assurance, and love that every child wants to hear."

Jason Curry
President of Texas Baptist Home for Children, adoptive dad

"If adoption is part of your family's story, this book is for you. It will help encourage your kiddos as well as help you assure them of the forever they have with you. This book is a must-have for your library."

Kasi and Shane Pruitt
Adoption and Foster Care Ministry Coordinator at Lakepointe Church, National Next Gen Director NAMB, author, adoptive parents

"*Together Forever* are words every adoptive child needs to not only hear, but to feel. In this book Charity Clayton has done a fantastic job portraying how the sweetest of moments between an adoptive mother and son can play out in order to bring not only healing to the child, but also to the mama. So often mothers need to be led to safety, as well, on the journey of raising children from hard places. It is in the very words of this book that safety is born between a parent and child. Every adoptive parent would benefit from reading this book with their family. What a wonderful way to connect with your child!"

Paula St. John
LCSW, TBRI practitioner, adoptive mom

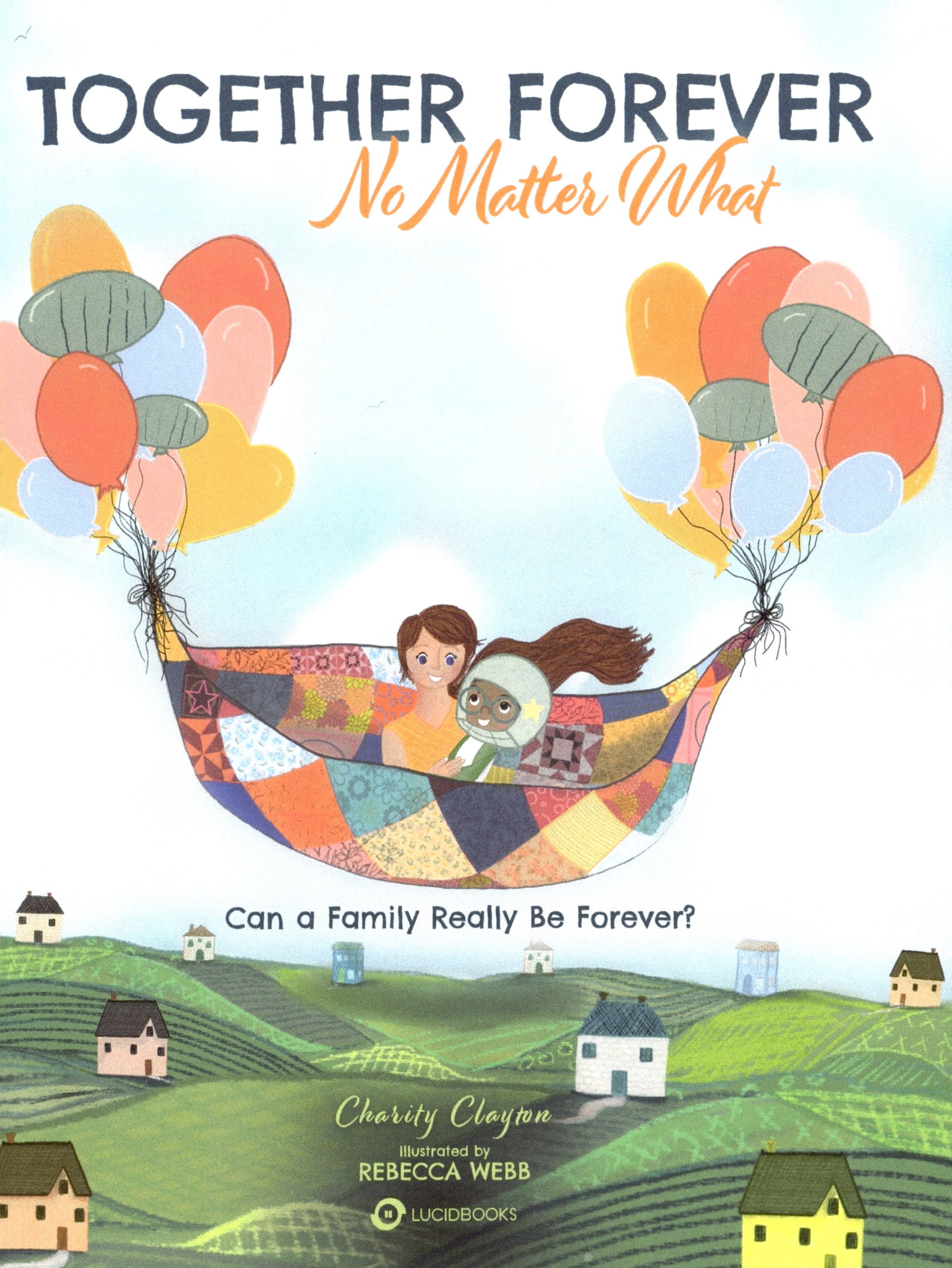

TOGETHER FOREVER
No Matter What
Can a Family Really Be Forever?
Charity Clayton
ILLUSTRATED BY
REBECCA WEBB
LUCIDBOOKS

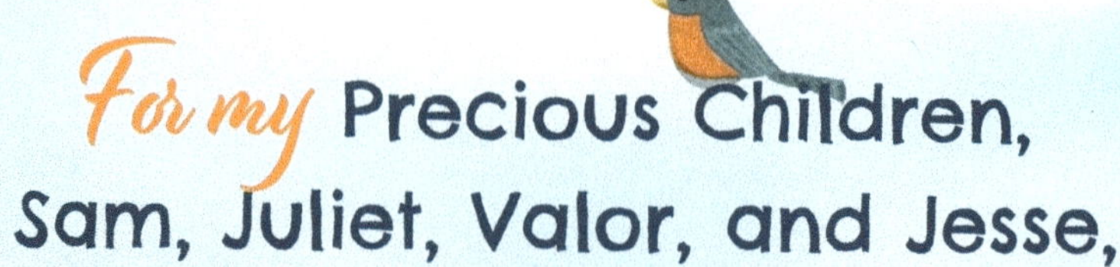

who have stuck with me as I make many parenting mistakes and love imperfectly. God has shown me great kindness in giving me you. I love you all so much.

Together Forever No Matter What

Can a Family Really Be Forever?

Copyright © 2023 by Charity Clayton

Illustrated by Rebecca Webb

Published by Lucid Books in
Houston, TX
www.LucidBooks.com

ISBN: 978-1-63296-629-2 (Hardback)
ISBN: 978-1-63296-984-2 (Paperback)
eISBN: 978-1-63296-630-8

Special Sales: Most Lucid Books titles are available in special quantity discounts.

Custom imprinting or excerpting can also be done to fit special needs.

Contact Lucid Books at Info@LucidBooks.com

Special THANKS

An enormous thank you to my incredible husband, Aaron, who has been by my side championing this book, helping me rearrange words to say just what I mean to, and cheering me on all the way. I would never have made it this far without you.

And to many friends and family who have been so excited as I attempt to help others in the way I've been helped on my journey, thank you! Your encouragement has meant more to me than you know!

Love you all!

To The PARENT

My earnest hope in writing this book is to help you, the adoptive parent, unearth the deep fear of abandonment in your child's heart. Every adoptee won't struggle with this fear to the same degree, but every one of them has experienced the tragic loss of their first family, and the impact on the child's life is profound.

Fear manifests itself in different ways. Often with our children, it shows up in the form of some negative behavior, and it frustrates us because we don't know what's driving it or how to change it. Left on that trajectory, we end up hopeless and despairing, and our children are left in their brokenness, not understanding how to function in a healthy family.

But, if we learn to meet our children where they are and seek to understand and validate their fears, we can build strong attachments and help to bring healing to their hearts. As that fear is brought to the surface, healing can begin. As you realize this legitimate fear is buried in your child's heart, you can start taking steps to make your child feel safe and secure with you.

My hope is that this book will help you tiptoe into this vulnerable space with your child in a way that allows them to safely explore scary feelings. You'll notice that the boy in the story starts with sillier questions, and they gradually get more honest as he feels more secure and realizes it's safe for him to explore these questions with his mom. She doesn't dismiss or dodge his hard questions but listens and responds with empathy, patiently reassuring him of her unconditional love and commitment to him.

As a follower of Jesus Christ, this picture reminds me so much of the gospel. Jesus doesn't choose us because we act right or have something really lovely in ourselves to offer Him. Often, I find, I'm just the opposite. I rebel against Him; I choose my own way because it feels safer. My trust in His goodness and good intentions toward me is weak. But He doesn't dismiss my fears. He doesn't harshly punish my disobedience. He stays near, gently calling to me, waiting to meet me in my weakness so that He can bring healing through a loving relationship.

This is the call. It goes beyond bringing vulnerable children into our homes and families. Following the example of Jesus, we are to lovingly meet our children where they are and lead them to healing. Psalm 73:22-24 paints this picture for us: "I was brutish and ignorant; I was like a beast toward you. Nevertheless, I am continually with you; you hold my right hand. You guide me with your counsel, and afterward, you will receive me to glory."

I am so grateful that this is the way God walks with me, and only when we have received this kind of care and love are we then able to give it freely to our children.

What a privilege it is to walk this road!

Mama,
will I be with
you forever?

Of course, *sweetie!*

We'll be together *forever,*
no matter what!

Even though I didn't grow in your tummy?
Yes, sweetheart. God brought you to us in a very special way.

We adopted you
because we wanted
to be with you
forever and ever.

Forever
and ever.

That's right.

Let me take a look at those
big chocolate eyes!

I want to look
at them forever!

Together forever
...even though I took Dad's shaver and cut Max's hair?

Yep, together forever.

I'm sure you'll remember
to ask next time.

Plus, I think Max really
likes his new haircut!

Even though I kicked over Sissy's tower today when I got mad?

Even then!

We're getting better at using our words every day.

It's hard to say how you feel, isn't it?

Even though I always forget to pick up my dirty underwear?

You don't always
forget, Kiddo, but yes.
Together forever,
even when you forget to pick up
your stinky undies!

Look at
Mama's eyes.
You're stuck
with us, Champ.

No matter
how you look
or where
you grew,

no matter
what you do,

we'll be
together forever,
no matter what!

Hmm.
Well, what if I build a rocket ship and run away to the moon?
To the moon

I'd build my own rocket ship
and never stop searching
until *I found you*.

Then we'd float home together.
You belong here with us.

What if I use up
all of your very berry
shampoo to make the
biggest bubble
bath ever?

Ha ha!
Yep, together forever.
In fact, let's do it!
It will be the bubbliest
bubble bath of all time!
Really?
Uh-huh.

What if I never run as fast as all of the other kids?
Will you still want me then?

We love you just the way you are.

We will always be
there to cheer you
on and give you a lift
when you need one!

No, *my love,*
but maybe you could hold my hand.
Even mamas get sad sometimes.

Well, what if I get sad and miss my first mom?

We can snuggle up together and be sad
about anything that hurts your heart.

It's okay for you to be sad, too;
but you never have to be sad alone.

Come here, bud.
No matter what
you feel

or what
you do,

no matter
whose shampoo
you use,

we'll be
together forever,
no matter what!

I got it.
Together. Forever . . .
no matter what.

You got it.
Goodnight, pumpkin.
Goodnight.

ALL DAY
EVERYDAY
Mama?
Yes?
If I forget,
will you tell me
again tomorrow?

Tomorrow
and the next day
and the day after that.
Forever and ever.

No matter what.

About THE AUTHOR

Charity was born in Dallas, Texas, and now resides in Waxahachie, Texas, where she and her husband, Aaron, have planted a church. They have four beautiful children, two adopted and two biological. Their difficult road in adoption led them to get the help and training they so desperately needed to connect with and parent their kids from hard places. After going through TCU's Hope Connect Camp, where they learned TBRI principles, Empowered to Connect Parent Training, and working with a child and family therapist in their home, Aaron and Charity are now certified parent trainers. Together, they find great joy in offering hope to adoptive parents, equipping them to understand and connect with their children.

About THE ILLUSTRATOR

Becca was born in Dallas, Texas. She has settled into a cozy home in the sweet town of Waxahachie, Texas, where she has found a freedom to create in a variety of ways, but her favorite thing to do is draw.

As a young girl, Becca knew she wanted to be an artist. After a missionary artist came to her church when she was a little girl, Becca decided she would be a missionary artist too, even though she had no clue what that meant. She began to draw everything in sight. And as she did, her parents encouraged her to keep drawing and nurtured her gift, buying her whatever supplies she needed.

Becca eventually became an artist, and after years teaching secondary art, Becca began a jewelry design business called Onyah Designs, which came to a close in 2020. Since then she has rested from that long season as an entrepreneur, and in that rest has re-discovered her love of drawing. She has found joy in getting back to her roots and using the gifts God has given her!

9 781632 966292